Supporting Children with Anxiety to Understand and Celebrate Difference

The 'Get to Know Me' resources aim to support children, with those around them, who may have additional/special educational needs. They are designed to empower the professionals and adults who support those with identified needs. Developed by child psychologist Dr Louise Lightfoot, the series includes activities specific to anxiety, depression and Obsessive Compulsive Disorder (OCD). In supporting the social and emotional health of students, it equips them with the ability to thrive, personally and academically.

This book has been created for key adults (teachers, therapists and parents) as a complement to the picture book and draw along versions of *Sammy Sloth* – a traditional narrative story exploring thoughts, feelings and sensations experienced by many children with anxiety.

The activities in this book offer practical tools and strategies to support the child and those around them, in addition to information specific to the condition to improve understanding of a child's needs to promote empathy and acceptance.

Picture book and draw along versions of *Sammy Sloth* are available separately, and as part of the Get to Know Me: Anxiety set.

Dr Louise Lightfoot is an Educational and Child Psychologist working with children and young people aged 0–25. She holds a BA in Educational Studies, MEd in the Psychology of Education and doctorate in Educational and Child Psychology. Louise has worked in a variety of settings ranging from mainstream schools to secure units and psychiatric facilities, and has a special interest in working to empower at risk or 'hard to reach' groups. As a person who suffers with Ehlers Danlos, stroke and dyslexia, she has a first-hand understanding of the frustrations and difficulties that accompany a specific physical or learning difficulty. Louise currently works as an HCPC registered Independent Psychologist. If you would like to discuss working with her, please contact Louise at: louise.lightfoot@hotmail.co.uk.

Catherine Hicks is an East Yorkshire artist, illustrator, wife and mother. She spent 13 years as a Registered Veterinary Nurse before injury and chronic illnesses led to her creative hobby becoming therapy. When Catherine and Louise were introduced, it was obvious they were kindred spirits and from there the Get to Know Me Series was born.

T0377407

GET TO KNOW ME SERIES

Series author: Dr Louise Lightfoot
Illustrated by: Catherine Hicks

The **'Get to Know Me'** series is a series of resources aimed at children with additional needs and the professionals who support them in the mainstream primary classroom. Each resource concentrates on a different condition and comprises of three titles, available separately.

A **traditional children's picture book** – designed to support the individual child but also to be used in whole class teaching, to encourage an empathetic and inclusive environment.

An **interactive work book**. This is a workbook version of the story in which indvidual children are encouraged to interact with the story in a creative way – through writing, drawing, scrap booking, collage, activities etc. (templates and cut outs will be made available online). Children are more likely to understand and process information if they have had to actively engage with it. The workbook will aid long-term recall and increase the level of understanding.

A **practitioner guide** created for key adults (teachers, therapists and parents) by a child psychologist, with activities specific to each condition. These activities will link to the books and offer practical tools and strategies to support the child and those around them in addition to the information specific to the condition to improve understanding of a child's needs to promote empathy and acceptance.

https://www.routledge.com/Get-To-Know-Me/book-series/GKM

Books included in this series:

Set 1 Get to Know Me: Anxiety
Available as a set and individual books

Book 1
Supporting Children with Anxiety to Understand and Celebrate Difference
A Get to Know Me Workbook and Guide for Parents and Practitioners
PB 978-0-8153-4941-9
eBook 978-1-351-16492-4

Book 2
Sammy Sloth
Get to Know Me: Anxiety
PB 978-0-8153-4953-2
eBook 978-1-351-16452-8

Book 3
Draw Along With Sammy Sloth
Get to Know Me: Anxiety

PB 978-0-8153-4942-6
eBook 978-1-351-16484-9

Set 2 Get to Know Me: Depression
Available as a set and individual books

Book 1
Supporting Children with Depression to Understand and Celebrate Difference
A Get to Know Me Workbook and Guide for Parents and Practitioners
PB 978-0-8153-4943-3
eBook 978-1-351-16480-1

Book 2
Silver Matilda
Get to Know Me: Depression
PB 978-0-8153-4945-7
eBook 978-1-351-16476-4

Book 3
Draw Along With Silver Matilda
Get to Know Me: Depression
PB 978-0-8153-4946-4
eBook 978-1-351-16472-6

Set 3 Get to Know Me: OCD
Available as a set and individual books

Book 1
Supporting Children with OCD to Understand and Celebrate Difference
A Get to Know Me Workbook and Guide for Parents and Practitioners
PB 978-0-8153-4948-8
eBook 978-1-351-16468-9

Book 2
Tidy Tim
Get to Know Me: OCD
PB 978-0-8153-4950-1
eBook 978-1-351-16460-3

Book 3
Draw Along With Tidy Tim
Get to Know Me: OCD
PB 978-0-8153-4951-8
eBook 978-1-351-16456-6

Supporting Children with Anxiety to Understand and Celebrate Difference

A Get to Know Me Workbook and Guide for Parents and Practitioners

Dr Louise Lightfoot

Illustrated by Catherine Hicks

Routledge
Taylor & Francis Group

LONDON AND NEW YORK

First published 2020
by Routledge
2 Park Square, Milton Park, Abingdon, Oxon OX14 4RN

and by Routledge
52 Vanderbilt Avenue, New York, NY 10017

Routledge is an imprint of the Taylor & Francis Group, an informa business

© 2020 Dr Louise Lightfoot & Catherine Hicks

The right of Dr Louise Lightfoot and Catherine Hicks to be identified as authors of this work
has been asserted by them in accordance with sections 77 and 78 of the Copyright,
Designs and Patents Act 1988.

British Library Cataloguing-in-Publication Data
A catalogue record for this book is available from the British Library

Library of Congress Cataloging-in-Publication Data
A catalog record has been requested for this book

ISBN: 978-0-8153-4941-9 (pbk)
ISBN: 978-1-351-16492-4 (ebk)

Typeset in Avant Garde Gothic Std
by Apex CoVantage, LLC

Visit the eResources: www.routledge.com/9780815349419

Contents

Acknowledgements

To Katrina my editor, thank you for taking a chance and sticking with us, especially during our particularly 'imperfectly flawed' moments! You have been a wonderful source of personal support and a professional wisdom.

Professor Kevin Woods for your (I often wondered if misguided) belief in me and continued support. Here's to being a square peg in a round hole.

The University of Manchester and the students of the Doctorate of Educational Psychology Course, in particular Jill and Ben Simpson, for their collaboration, perspective and belief.

Huge thank you for the contributions of: Dr Lindsay 'grammar' Kay, Dr Katie Pierce, Dr Richard Skelton, Dr Rachael Hornsby, Dr Rachel Lyons and Jade Charelson for their professional insight, unwavering friendship, invaluable contribution and time. You really are the Waitrose of Psychologists (quality wise, not overpriced!).

Thank you to all my family and friends who have endured numerous versions of these books and for their support during the periods in which I was very ill and gained tenacity from believing I could make something good come out of it all.

To Erin and Drew for being excellent guinea pigs and the source of great inspiration. To Owen for being a friend to me at 13 and 35 with admittedly slightly improved cooking skills. To Dianne Davies for her experience, support and knowledge of the area which helped more than you could know.

A huge thank you to Tim Watson for your supervision, guidance and support. You have helped me realise my potential when I couldn't see it in myself. You are an excellent critical friend, fountain of knowledge and all round lovely person!

Thanks to Catherine Hicks, my illustrator, the gin to my tonic! Perhaps in finding each other we made two slightly broken people whole.

To Jenni O'Sullivan-Ward, Isabella Hickling and Sharon Pellegrini for all your last-minute help!

Thanks to Dr Paula Muir for your insight, guidance and Kefir.

Thanks for my Dad for always believing in me and constantly filling my freezer and thanks to my big brother John, who annoyed me as a child and who has always been there for me as an adult.

To the Hickling family, I couldn't have wished to marry into a better family, your support love and acceptance of me as a Scouser is forever appreciated.

Thank you to Jonathan Merrett, the copy editor, for his patience and flexibility and to Leah Burton, my Editorial Assistant, for her help along the way.

Finally, a huge thank you to Gillian Steadman, my Senior Production Editor, who is the yin to my yang. Couldn't have done this without you!

Introduction to the Resource Pack

This guidebook is for the parents/carers and professionals supporting children who may be experiencing difficulties associated with anxiety. This resource has been created to:

◆ raise awareness

◆ explore the presentation, frequency and potential sources of support around a specific issue

◆ explain and find a common language to use around an issue to those experiencing it and those around them

◆ create empathy and help to normalise behaviours and feelings

◆ help children make sense of their feelings

◆ provide some strategies that may offer immediate help and support to children

◆ signpost when appropriate.

This book was written with children with anxiety in mind and it is hoped they will relate to the thoughts, feelings, behaviours and experiences of Sammy. However, children with a range of needs may benefit from the story, and particularly if they experience any of the following:

◆ changeable mood

◆ over prediction of their behaviour on outcomes

◆ an increased sense of responsibility

◆ predicting and fear and fear of failure

◆ persistent and ruminating thoughts

◆ low self-esteem and self-efficacy.

WHAT IS ANXIETY?

Anxiety can be described as a type of fear usually associated with the thought of a threat or something going wrong in the future, but can also arise from something happening right now.

One in six people in the past week have experienced anxiety and this is therefore one of the more common mental health problems.[1] It is likely that many individuals do not seek help for

---

1 https://adaa.org/living-with-anxiety/children/anxiety-and-depression

anxiety, meaning many remain without diagnosis or treatment and the actual numbers may be much higher.

SIGNS AND SYMPTOMS OF ANXIETY

It is normal to feel anxious about everyday things as life is full of potential stressful events. It might be that there can be a single trigger or event that raises anxiety levels, an accumulation of things that increase anxiety levels, including exams, work deadlines, how we think we look, going on a first date or whether we feel safe travelling home late at night. Sometimes anxiety levels can increase for no known reason. This is known as Generalised Anxiety Disorder (GAD) and is how Sammy experiences anxiety in the book.

Anxiety has a strong effect on us because it's one of our natural survival responses. It causes our mind and body to speed up to prepare us to respond to an emergency.

Some of the physical things that might happen are:

◆ rapid and/or irregular heartbeat

◆ fast breathing

◆ weakened or tense muscles

◆ sweating

◆ churning stomach or loose bowels

◆ dizziness

◆ dry mouth.

Anxiety also has a psychological impact, which can include:

◆ trouble sleeping

◆ lack of concentration

◆ feeling irritable

◆ feeling depressed

◆ loss of self-confidence.

It can be hard to break this cycle, but you can learn to feel less worried and to cope with your anxiety so it doesn't stop you enjoying life.

WHAT ARE THE CAUSES OF ANXIETY?

Feelings of anxiety can be caused by lots of things and vary according to what you're worried about and how you act when you feel apprehensive. They depend on lots of things such as:

◆ your genes

◆ how you were brought up

◆ your life experiences

◆ the way you learn and cope with things.

Just knowing what makes you anxious and why can be the first steps to managing anxiety. Someone with anxiety might have thoughts like . . .

If I don't do this, something bad will happen

I want to do these things, but I have to

I'll try and keep these thoughts things hidden as they are strange

There is a wrong and a right way to do something

I do not understand why other people cannot see the 'right' way to do something

If I can't act out my compulsion, I will feel bad

I'm afraid of dirt or unclean things, I must watch out

If people do things differently to me or interfere with my way it makes me anxious

Not being able to complete a compulsion makes me feel bad.

SUPPORTING CHILDREN IN THE CLASSROOM

Below are some behaviours you might notice pupils with anxiety displaying (this list is not exhaustive):

◆ appears tired, with poor attention and concentration

◆ has difficulties remembering information and following instructions

◆ has difficulties starting and finishing tasks

◆ a high need for reassurance

◆ apparent refusal to follow adult instruction

◆ walking out of the classroom or away from an adult when they are speaking to them

◆ underachievement

◆ aggression

◆ taking excessive amounts of time to complete tasks/incomplete work

◆ frequently feeling unwell with stomach ache/headaches

◆ perfectionism (this may feed into low self-esteem)

◆ fear of failure or getting things 'wrong'

◆ frozen/inactive within the classroom.

HOW TO SUPPORT PUPILS WITH ANXIETY IN SCHOOL

◆ be available and give time to listen to pupils' concerns

◆ empathise, let them know that they are not alone with the difficult/uncomfortable feeling

◆ know about the symptoms of anxiety for your pupil

◆ communicate effectively with parents/ carers

◆ work alongside multiple agencies as needed to better understand the pupil and their needs

◆ create an Individual Education Plan (IEP) or similar based on the pupil's needs and review this regularly (e.g. each half term)

◆ differentiate tasks and have realistic expectations

◆ help pupils to start their work

◆ regularly check in with the pupil as they may not be able to ask for help when they need it the most

◆ break down tasks into smaller, more manageable chunks so as not to overwhelm the child

◆ allow frequent breaks and consider a system to allow the pupil to communicate their need for a break without drawing attention to them

◆ have a 'safe' adult the pupil can access when experiencing difficulties with their anxiety

◆ have a designated 'safe' place the young person can access when needed

◆ carefully consider seating plans (depending on the triggers for the particular pupil)

◆ educate all students about diversity (via specifically targeted Circle times or within Personal Social Health Economic Education (PSHE).

Please be mindful that any accommodations made for pupils with anxiety may only be temporary and can be reduced or removed as they make progress. All accommodations must be developed in collaboration with the pupil, their parents/carers and any other relevant agencies involved.

ADVICE FOR PARENTS

Anxiety is a natural emotion. After all, we've all felt anxious at some points in our lives, whether it be temporary or more long term. We have this emotion to let us know that something isn't right, and we should do something about it. However, your child may feel anxious for lots of different reasons and not necessarily have the insight or recognition to be able to talk about it in detail. Their response when feeling this anxiety may be to try and avoid the situation or rely on an adult (i.e. you) to manage it for them. By avoiding what is causing the anxiety, this temporarily makes them feel better, but leads to a reinforcement of them thinking that they cannot cope with it, and stops them from being able to develop skills necessary to manage the situation in the future.

While you may see your child's anxiety expressed through avoiding situations and appearing nervous or worried, you may also notice the effects it has on their sleep, feeling stomach aches or headaches, and can also be expressed as strong feelings of irritability. We can often see a child's anxiety within different contexts. Some children experience Generalised Anxiety Disorder (GAD) and appear avoidant and withdrawn to a wide range of situations; other children experience Social Anxiety and are very self-conscious and fearful of others seeing them negatively, and some children experience Separation Anxiety where they feel distress at being away from their family and often worry that something bad will happen.

With the right support, anxiety is very treatable and there is a lot you and your child can do. Early intervention is key; and we know that the sooner we get a plan in place to help a child anxiety, the quicker and more sustained their improvement will be.

THINGS TO CONSIDER

◆ *Support.* If you think your child has anxiety, it is important to seek help. There are a lot of professionals who help children with anxiety and there are a lot of excellent techniques and approaches which we know work very well. Specialist support can be accessed through your General Practitioner (GP) and, if your child is older, they may wish to speak to the GP alone. Support can also be found through school, and the school SENCO will likely have supported lots of children experiencing anxiety in the past.

◆ *Calm and open.* Hearing your child describing their symptoms, especially their most feared and anxious thoughts, maybe upsetting or appear completely unfounded. Try to prepare yourself so that you can remain calm and accepting, and try not to jump in and reassure straight away. By simply listening and empathising, you can help your child open up and talk honestly about what they are experiencing.

◆ *Knowledge is power.* The more you can learn about anxiety, the better you'll be able to support your child. There are some excellent books, websites and videos available (see end of this section), and try to get recommendations from a professional or school SENCO where you can.

◆ *Seeking reasons.* There is no definitive answer as to why your child has anxiety, and it is often a combination of physiological and environmental factors. While we often have an instinct to want to know the cause, what matters most is what we do to support our child to recovery.

◆ *Positive parenting.* Anxiety is not an indication of poor parenting. Sometimes, it can even be that our best intentions and protective nature (i.e. natural positive parental instincts) have meant that we have accommodated these anxieties and need to look at how we can help our child to grow through their experiences.

◆ *Consistency.* If our child has anxiety, we need to support them over time. There will always be things each day which make them feel more or less anxious, calmer or happier. This is important to know and recognise because there will be times when we think our efforts aren't working because they've had an anxious day, but we are helping. There will be times when our child appears really happy and calm, but we need to continue to build their skills to make sure their anxiety doesn't return. When we start, let's do this properly, and that means that we're committed to being consistent, good days or bad (for both our child and ourselves).

◆ *Reassurance giving.* When we provide reassurance, we are accommodating our child. That is, we can remove their anxiety on this occasion, but if we're not around then they still do not have the sills to manage this by themselves. While it can be hard, try not to offer reassurance or 'accommodate' the anxiety. As a parent you want to reduce your child's distress, but reassurance can only reduce their anxiety for a short time, and it will return just as strong next time. Of course, there will be times and places when you will feel the need to reassure, but it's important we help the child to grow through supporting them through the experience, rather than managing it for them.

◆ *Happy parents, happy kids.* Anxiety can be very distressing and disruptive for the whole family. But you are the most important role model for your child. If you feel stressed out, anxious or just fed up, then it can be very difficult to support your child. Sometimes we need to take a step back and think about our own wellbeing, and making sure that we have enough 'down time', rest, relaxation, fun, and friends. Doing so is important so that we are in the best place to help our children.

◆ *Talking to school.* Telling your child's school can be very beneficial, as they have a responsibility to support your child, and will likely have a lot of experience of working with children experiencing anxiety. There are a number of guides for schools, and the ANXIETY UK and ANXIETY Action Parent Guides include information for parents about working with school staff. However, the decision to inform school or not of your child's ANXIETY will depend on your and your child's own circumstances, preferences and the severity of their symptoms. Whatever you decide, it's important to involve your child in this decision, to make sure that they feel in control.

TREATMENT

◆ *Mindfulness.* You may have heard about mindfulness as it has become a very popular meditation technique, which has especially been shown to improve anxiety. This has many parts to it, but helps to identify feelings and learn skills to manage both these feelings and stop any negative thoughts which may be spiralling. Learning mindfulness is training an ability like any other, and is often compared to starting running training. It is important to recognise that those of us that find it hard are often those that need to practice it more. What I mean by this is, please don't give up if you find yourself or your child only being able to do a couple of minutes to start. That is just your starting point, and you will improve with training. Mindfulness can be practised with your child through the use of apps, video and audio guidance. Resources such as the book *Sitting Still Like a Frog* by Eline Snel, apps like Headspace, and websites by Breathworks are all useful start points to explore mindfulness both for yourself and your child.

◆ *CBT.* Cognitive Behavioural Therapy is a form of 'talking therapy' which has been shown to be very effective in the treatment of anxiety. CBT helps people understand how thoughts (e.g. I will get hurt), feelings (e.g. anxiety) and behaviours (e.g. I'm going to hide away) are linked. This helps to be able to support the child to change their thoughts or behaviours, knowing that this will reduce their anxiety in the future. This is a very effective approach which can be adapted to meet the needs of young children, to older teenagers. CBT can be accessed through a professional, but there are also some very good resources, workbooks and guides for parents using CBT approaches such as *Starving the Anxiety Gremlin* workbook by Kate Collins-Donnelly.

◆ *Medication* may also be offered, usually anti-depressant medications (Selective Seretonin Reuptake Inhibitors; SSRI), which may help reduce anxiety so as to better engage with Cognitive Behavioural Therapy (CBT). Having a discussion about the pros and cons of such medication, and the potential side effects with your GP is important (the NICE Guidelines are available online and provide national guidance for England and Wales on the appropriate treatment and care of people with anxiety, based on the best available evidence).

◆ *Goal setting.* When we have talked to our child about anxiety, the first and most important step is to set goals. For this, we want a long-term goal (e.g. feel confident to play with everyone on the playground), and a short-term goal (e.g. feel confident to talk to one friend at lunch time). This is important for us and our child to see the person they want to be (i.e. long-term goal), and what we're currently working towards (i.e. short-term goal), which increases motivation and provides a clarity to all those around our child of what we can do to support them with this. Sometimes we may feel that our short-term goals are too small, but small-step progress (i.e. one little thing we can change tomorrow) is great because it provides a lot of successes. So smaller targets can be a great thing to build confidence, and see quicker progression in the long run. When we've set these, it's important that someone is there to prepare, role-play and then coach your child through that situation.

SUPPORTING CHILDREN ON AN INDIVIDUAL LEVEL

It is important to be patient and empathic when supporting children who struggle with anxiety. What may seem insignificant to an adult may be the cause of great anxiety for the child. The following general approaches may be useful when supporting children and when working through the worksheets and resources provided.

Assessing the needs of each individual child and working safely within these limits is crucial. For some children, simply reading about a character that displays similar behaviours can have a positive impact in 'normalising' their behaviours and feelings. The activities in the resource pack are designed in such a way that the activities early on in the pack are not emotionally demanding and are designed to be fun and engaging and to consolidate their understanding of the story. During these activities the children are asked to focus on and consider the characters behaviours and feelings rather than their own. As the pack progresses, the child is expected to relate their own thoughts, feelings and behaviours to that of the characters therefore gaining insight into their own needs. Finally, the child is encouraged to consider and develop coping strategies which may relieve their anxiety and support them to manage their behaviour. It is important that each child works at their own pace and is supported by a skilled adult who is able to assess the child's needs, limits and have plans as to how to help the child manage uncomfortable feelings resulting from 1:1 work. It is good practice to:

◆ Let the child set the pace.

◆ Work in a non-judgemental manner and refrain from interpreting pictures and content unless suitably qualified.

◆ Recognise that every child is different and will have different needs and interests. It is important to modify your approach depending on the age (chronological and developmental) ethnicity and relevant social/economic factors of the child.

◆ It is useful to consider each child's individual learning style, literacy and cognitive abilities as well as their emotional literacy. Some children do not enjoy reading/writing and may be reluctant to engage in what may be perceived as 'work'. This resource pack has been designed to engage particularly creative or active children through craft based/practical activities.

◆ It may be useful to start and end a session with 'problem-free talk' which includes activities that can be used to help the adult build rapport with the child and discover what is important to them.

◆ Do not let the activities you choose be restricted by the child's age. Some teenagers will enjoy what seems like 'childish' activities (e.g. dot to dot) while some younger children may be more able. It is always useful to start work with an activity that is non-threatening and well within their capabilities to build confidence and support the child to feel safe.

◆ It is useful to consider the role of the child's existing support network (home life and within school) and to collaborate with such persons in order to reinforce and advance the work taking place within sessions.

◆ It is important to come to sessions prepared with a back-up plan and to get to know if a child has a known interest, to include this at the end of a session or if a session becomes difficult or if the child is not easily engaged.

◆ It is important to reflect on (and if available, have supervision with a trained professional) as to the progress of any 1:1 work and to tailor your approaches accordingly.

◆ It is good practice to bring the child's earlier work to subsequent sessions so that you can refer back to it, chart progress and praise/show value in the work achieved.

◆ It is useful for most children to know when sessions are happening, what they will entail and how long they will last. It is particularly important for children with anxiety and control issues to know in advance of sessions what is to be expected of them and for any change in a set timetable or cancellation to be shared with the child as soon as possible.

USEFUL LINKS

The following organisations provide user friendly materials and guides for parents to explain what anxiety is (what symptoms to look out for, the difference between types of anxieties), recommended treatments, and how best to support your child at home and school:

NHS Choices: www.nhs.uk

Mental Health and Growing Up Factsheet: Worries and anxieties – helping children to cope: www.rcpsych.ac.uk

YoungMinds Parent Helpline: 0808 802 5544

Child Line: www.childline.org.uk 0800 1111

Anxiety UK: www.anxietyuk.org.uk 08444 775 774

SANE: www.sane.org.uk 03003047000

Anxiety UK: www.anxietyuk.org.uk 08444 775 774

I Speak (Selective Mutism) www.ispeak.org.uk

HELPFUL BOOKS

K. D. Buron, *When My Worries Get Too Big! A Relaxation Book for Children*

E. Snel, *Sitting Still Like a Frog: Mindfulness Exercises for Kids (and Their Parents)*

K. Collins-Donnelly, *Starving the Anxiety Gremlin: A Cognitive Behavioural Therapy Workbook*

K. Martinez and M. Tompkins, *My Anxious Mind: A Teen's Guide to Managing Anxiety and Panic*

V. Ironside, *The Huge Bag of Worries*

J. Evans, *Little Meerkat's Big Panic*

The Margot Sunderland story books

Chapter 1

Feelings generator

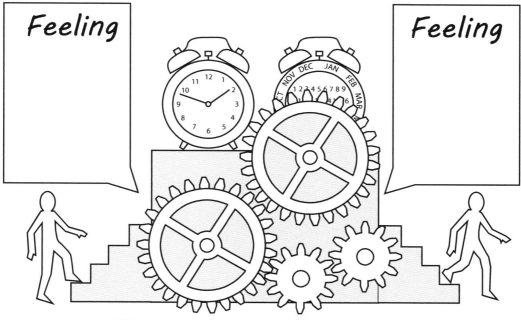

The Feelings Generator

The feelings generator can help us to understand the feelings that maybe causing our behaviour. There are often many different names used to describe the same feeling and this can make it tricky to understand and express how we are feeling.

Below is an example of how the feeling 'angry' can be described in different ways:

Angry = mad, grumpy, frustrated, annoyed, irritated, furious, cross, fuming, raging

Can you think of anymore?

Continue to find others names for the following feelings:

◆ Scared

◆ Anxious

◆ Happy

◆ Ashamed

◆ Proud

◆ Sad

◆ Bad

Do you notice anything about the terms? Do some seem stronger than others? Do some fit into more than one category? Having a big emotional vocabulary can help to express our feelings and needs to others.

Using the flash cards provided overleaf, write down the different feelings and see if, when you mix them all together, you are able to group these feelings back with the initial term. For example, all feelings related to angry would be placed under the 'angry' flash card.

Additional activities:

◆ Photocopy the flash cards so there are two sets of each feeling. Use these to play 'snap'. This helps to improve word recognition.

◆ Place the photocopied flash cards on a table in a random order paying close attention to the cards. Then turn them over and pick up two cards displaying the same feeling if you can remember where the cards are! Set aside each matched 'pair'. This can be played alone or with others. The person with the most pairs wins! This game improves memory and attention.

◆ Mix the cards up and use to play charades. Each person should pick a card and act out that feeling whilst the other players guess. This can be done in a pair or in teams. This is useful in supporting emotional intelligence and for recognising behaviours in ourselves and others.

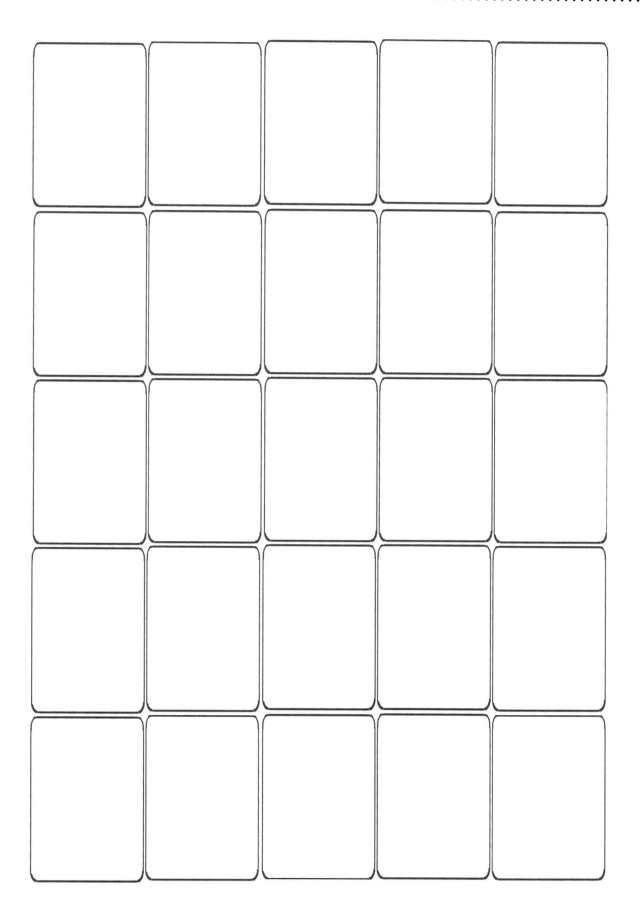

Chapter 2

Blow up your worries!

Materials needed: Balloons and pens.

Purpose: Often children with difficulties around anxiety and control suffer to cope with these feelings and they can build up so they feel unmanageable. Helping them to confront their problems in a visual and practical way can help to put these feelings into perspective and make them seem more manageable.

Instructions: Give them a balloon and ask them to write a list of their current worries down. For example, the list of worries might be around school refusal. This might generate a list such as fear of:

◆ Falling behind

◆ Not getting any qualifications

◆ Losing friends

◆ Not being able to get a job

◆ Disappointing parents

◆ Not being able to buy a house or have a car/nice things

◆ Being more anxious and needing to see a psychiatrist or to be made to take tablets.

Draw the word 'worries' on the balloon and ask them to blow up the balloon, naming each worry with each breath (if they are unable to generate a list themselves write down a list of things Tidy Tim may have (for example, not having friends, not knowing how to play, feeling like he has too much to do etc.). Keep blowing up the balloon until it pops. Explain to the child that if we don't find a way to manage our feelings they can overwhelm us and make us 'pop'. This might look like crying, having a panic attack, having a physical response such as shaking or becoming angry and shouting or destroying objects or attacking people. Then ask the child to write down on different balloons individual worries. Write down a list of what is worrying the child and try to help them to break it down.

EXAMPLE: FALLING BEHIND.

The worries around this might be:

◆ Missing school means missing work

◆ Missing work means not feeling confident in class and being scared to ask for help

◆ Being afraid to seem 'stupid'

◆ Feeling like they are so behind they can't catch up

◆ Knowing that missing school is making it worse and feeling guilty for allowing things to get worse.

Repeat the exercise (blowing up the balloon whist naming the individual worries until it pops).

Now go through the list and see if any of the things can be made better, who can help and what strategies can be employed to reduce anxiety. Some things will remain a worry and that's ok.

◆ Missing school means missing work: can school provide work that can be done at home or a tutor to summarise and prioritise so it is manageable?

◆ Missing work means not feeling confident in class and being scared to ask for help: are there examples of other children who have had time off through sickness for example? Try to normalise feeling anxious and make arrangements with staff to 'check' that the child understands the task and adopt a nonverbal way for them to ask for help - for example placing a red pencil on the table if they are stuck or feeling anxious.

◆ Being afraid to seem 'stupid': use an exercise and approaches such as the compliment cards to identify and reflect back to the child their strengths. Get them to draw a list of their strengths and use any evidence of previous achievement to combat these negative feelings (e.g, awards, good grades).

◆ Feeling like they are so behind they can't catch up: explaining that this is normal and many people feel this way after being absent from school or work.

◆ Knowing that missing school is making it worse and feeling guilty for allowing things to get worse: explain that starting to address their fears and making small but manageable attempts to return will automatically make them feel better as they are taking control of the situation.

Ask the child the blow up the balloon again and to name the things they are still worried about. Hopefully the balloon will be smaller and they can let the balloon go rather than letting it get so big that it pops on its own.

Outcome: This exercise is useful in showing how worries, without intervention, can seem so big they can become paralysing. Showing how breaking them down and thinking of solutions and ways to seek support can be empowering and reduce anxiety. This helps the child to take back control and devise strategies for coping without dismissing or invalidating their worries. This exercise helps to give the child tools to recognise and tackle their worries in a proactive way and to find a way to move forward in a productive manner.

Chapter 3

The ball of worries

Materials needed: Several different coloured pieces of string, wool, or ribbon.

Purpose: Some children become overwhelmed with the various worries and intrusive thoughts they experience. They start to feel as though they can't begin to figure out their problems because they don't know where to start. The ball of worries activity introduces children to a practical coping strategy to make thoughts and worries appear more manageable.

Instructions: Label each different coloured string as an intrusive thought or 'worry'. Jumble them up into a ball. Talk about how it feels to look at them all jumbled up (e.g. confusing, overwhelming, hard to see or know where to start). Then how pulling them apart makes them easier to see and appear more manageable.

Outcome: Children are encouraged to see that it is easier to find solutions and sources of support when focusing on one worry at a time. When they start to feel overwhelmed by their worries, they can be reminded of the ball of worries and encouraged to 'untangle' them and identify one worry to work on.

Chapter 4

Feelings sorter

Often our behaviour gives us clues about how we are feeling deep down. Sometimes we might act angry when we are actually feeling worried. Use the feeling sorter to enter 'in' a behaviour and try to figure out what the 'underlying' feeling might be.

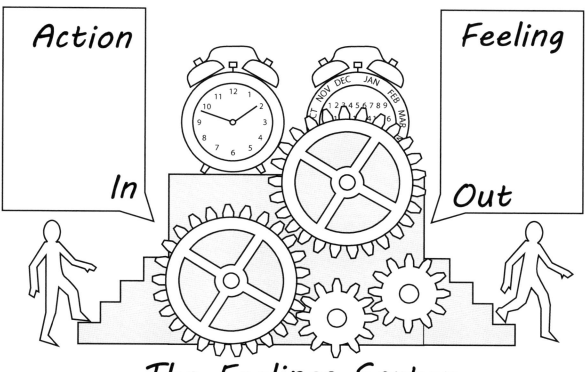

The Feelings Sorter

Chapter 5

Using puppets and play to explore emotions

Puppets can be a great way to engage children in play as they are not only fun but give children a feeling of distance from what they might feel comfortable saying and what the puppet is able to say on their behalf. You might find that a child will reveal more when talking 'through a puppet' that when asked directly. It should also be noted that some children use puppets to simply play and use their imagination.

HOW TO MAKE A PUPPET

Materials needed:

Paper towel holders or toilet paper cardboard holder

Wiggly eyes

Wool

Colourful paper

Paint

Scissors

Blue tack

Glue.

Directions:

◆ Cover the toilet or paper towel cardboard holder with coloured paper or paint. You may want to use different colours for the face, body and clothing.

◆ Use the 'emotion tracker' to make different facial expressions that can be switched on and off using blue tack as appropriate

◆ Choose wool to make the hair and glue it on the top of the paper towel holder/toilet paper holder.

◆ Decorate the puppet! This can be done by drawing or painting on clothes, or adding stickers.

◆ A large lollipop stick can be added at the base of the puppet so it can be held up by the child.

Puppets can be used in various ways. These include:

◆ To engage shy or reluctant children to speak out.

◆ To enact past experience or confrontations and to replay them after reflection and to act out 'what could' have been done differently.

◆ To 'practice' difficult situations with children so they can rely on a series of 'scripts' to deal with difficult or novel situations. Not only are 'scripts' useful in helping the child to act appropriately in the moment but merely practicing the scripts can often alleviate anxiety.

For example, when a child asks 'what's wrong with you?' a script might be:

'I find new situations and change hard to deal with. I might need some help at these times. Can I help you in anyway?'

It can be useful to practice what can be unhelpful comments, although they might be said with good intentions.

For example when a child reports 'feeling sad' an unsuitable script might be:

'Don't be silly, what do you have to sad about, it's your birthday next week and you'll gets lots of presents, you should be very happy, some children don't get any presents!'

It can, therefore, be useful to build empathy and understanding not only with those experiencing difficulties, but those around them. When we are feeling emotionally vulnerable, what people say can have more impact than usual. It is therefore important to be sensitive and considerate with language and with actions and to validate and empathise with those suffering with poor mental health.

Chapter 6

Colour your feelings

◆ Pick colours that represents different emotions you feel.

◆ Use colours to represent how you might feel in different situations.

◆ Where do you feel things in your body?

Chapter 7

Compliment cards, part 1

Materials needed: Paper or note cards and pen.

Purpose: Often children with difficulties around control and anxiety suffer with low self-esteem. They may experience feelings of being different and feeling 'strange' and may struggle relate to their peers. Using compliment cards is a way of reflecting back to the child their strengths and enabling them to see how many people value them.

Instructions: Give the compliment cards to significant adults (and when appropriate other children) in the child's life (for example, teachers, parents, siblings, lunch time supervisors) and ask them to write a compliment about them. The compliment may relate to their personal qualities, an academic subject they engage well with or a specific talent or skill they have. The adult then reads the compliment to the child and they are asked to guess who wrote that compliment about them. The compliment cards game is played regularly or until the child can correctly identify the author of the compliment.

Outcome: Using these cards not only gives child the opportunity to feel appreciated and valued but they are able to see the range of people available to them. It might be that one particular feature appears in many of the compliment cards and this can be identified as a particular strength which is confirmed by many people making this more likely to be accepted. If a variety of different compliments are offered by those taking part, this can be used to show the child just how many good qualities they have. Asking the child to 'guess' who the compliments are from rather than just being asked to read them, not only makes the activity more fun but also makes the process more comfortable for children who may struggle to receive direct compliments due to poor self-esteem. Placing the focus on guessing the source of the compliment changes the focus of the game initially whilst continuing to allow the child to hear the compliments. The repetition of this game is designed to ensure that the child hears the compliments over and over, supporting the child to believe them and increasing self-esteem.

Chapter 8

Compliment cards, part 2

Materials needed: Paper or note cards and pen.

Purpose: Often children with difficulties with control and feel there is a 'right' way of doing things. The right way is typically theirs! Subsequently they may struggle to see things from the perspective of others or to value views when they are in opposition to their own. This may lead them to experience feelings of being different or 'strange' and they may not relate well to their peers. Working with the child to create compliment cards is a way of encouraging empathy, supporting the child to see good qualities in others and fostering flexible thinking.

Instructions: Give the child blank compliment cards and ask them to write down compliments about significant adults (and when appropriate other children) in their life (for example, teachers, parents, siblings, lunch time supervisors). The compliments may relate to their personal qualities or a specific talent or skill they have. If the child is confident enough, they can be supported to read the compliment to the relevant person along with a compliment about someone else. The child then asks the person to identify which compliment relates to them. If they are not confident enough to do this, they can keep the collection of cards which can be reviewed to remind the child that we all have different strengths.

Outcome: The participants are not only given the opportunity to identify good qualities in others but are then able to practice sharing this appreciation with others. This allows the child not only to improve their social skills but encourages them to see the diversity in people and to appreciate their skills. It is hoped that through such an activity the child can, through appreciating others, learn to appreciate themselves and their special skills and qualities.

Chapter 9

The bridge to success

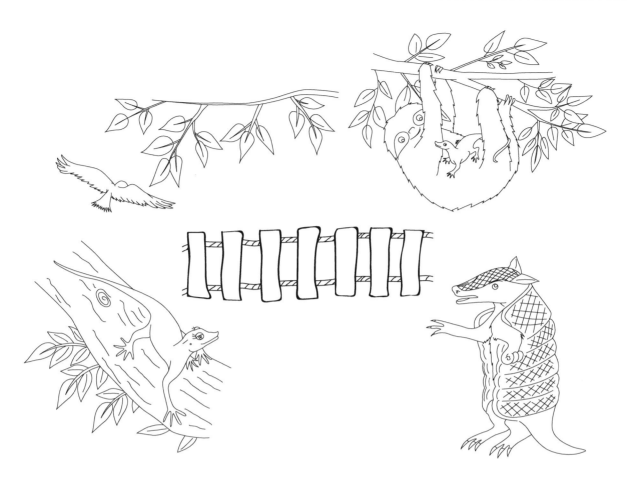

This game helps children to identify elements of the child's life that they would like to succeed in and helps them to plan (with the help of metaphor) a course of action that will help them move forward.

In all real-life situations there are forces and circumstances that impact either positively or negatively on any given outcome. This game helps the child the look at the impact of outside influences be it positive it or negative.

The bridge to success represents positive steps that need to be taken by the child in order to get to the other side or the desired changes. This may involve engaging in a particular behaviour e.g. attending school, refraining from a particular behaviour e.g. abusing drugs, and seeking support for example school counsellor. These would all constitute 'steps' across the bridge.

'Threats' to achieving these goals should be identified to allow the person the best possible chance of tackling and avoiding such threats. Threats may include: peer pressure, addiction and their own self-belief.

Each threat and step should be discussed and planned for with a supportive adult to increase the likelihood of achieving their goals, and giving them the tools and the confidence they need to successfully cross the bridge.

Chapter 10

Always, never, everybody

When someone is feeling low it can be hard not to generalise negative feelings and to use language that supports staying in a negative frame of mind. Ask them to try and spot when they use phrases like:

◆ always,

◆ everybody,

◆ nobody,

◆ everywhere,

◆ no one,

◆ always,

◆ never,

and to write them down, it might be a useful idea to collect these 'statements' in a jar for reference as an aid to monitor progress. It may also be helpful to ask the child to try and think of a different way of phrasing their feelings without using the above mentioned words.

Tracking the use of such language can be a useful way of indicating good and bad days and showing progress.

Chapter 11

The miracle question

Imagine you went to sleep you and all the difficult feelings you had went away. When you woke up . . .

◆   What would it be like?

◆   Who would be there?

◆   How would your day start?

◆   What would happen next?

◆   What else . . .?

◆   What you are doing?

Draw or discuss.

Chapter 12

The wrong is right game

Materials needed: Quiz questions

Purpose: Some children have very inflexible thinking and believe there is a right or a wrong way to do things. Anxiety can increase when they are not allowed to do things in the 'right' way and may react negatively when making a mistake. This game enables children to practice being 'wrong' in a safe environment.

Instructions: Children are quizzed about the book they have read and are only allowed to answer with an incorrect statement. Readers are encouraged to use their imagination and be creative with their answers.

EXAMPLE

What type of creature is Sammy?

Incorrect answer: Sloth

Correct answer: Horse

Outcome: Readers are not only given the opportunity to consolidate their understanding of the book but are able to practice being 'wrong'. Not only is this fun as children are encouraged to give creative answers but in going through the motions when being incorrect in a safe way, this can be generalised to other situations and help to reduce anxiety and promote flexible thinking.

Chapter 13

Sammy Sloth's Activity Book

Sammy Sloth's Activity Book

Colour In

Sam and Livy

Sam and Livy's Dot-to-Dot

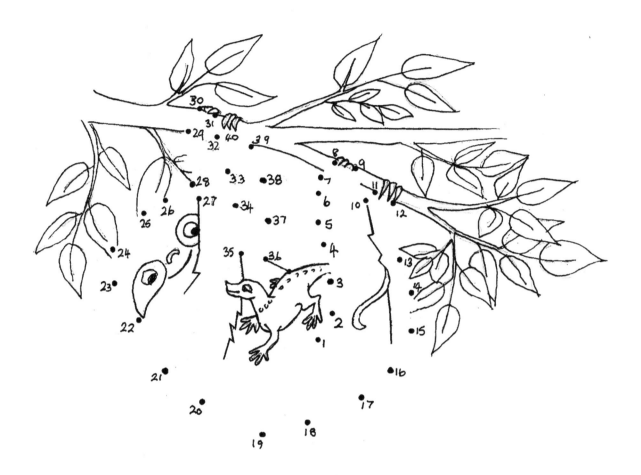

Join the dots in order
to complete the picture,
then you can colour it in.

A   B   C   D   E

Sam wants to climb back up to
the sloths' tree top home.
Which vine should Sam use?
A, B, C, D or E?

Sammy Sloth's Crossword

Clues Across

2: Be anxious (5)
4: De-stress, chill out (5)
5: Anna is one of these (9)
5: The name of the sloth (3)
8: All by yourself (5)
9: Emotions, sensations (8)
12 : The people you live with
14 : Difficulty, something to solve
15 : Glad, joyful (5)

Clues Down

1: People you like to spend time with (7)
3: Anxious, worried (8)
7: The name of the armadillo (4)
8: Sorry, embarrassed (7)
10: Livy is one of these (6)
11: Sam is one of these (5)
13 : the name of the lizard (4)

Sammy Sloth's Crossword (extra clues)

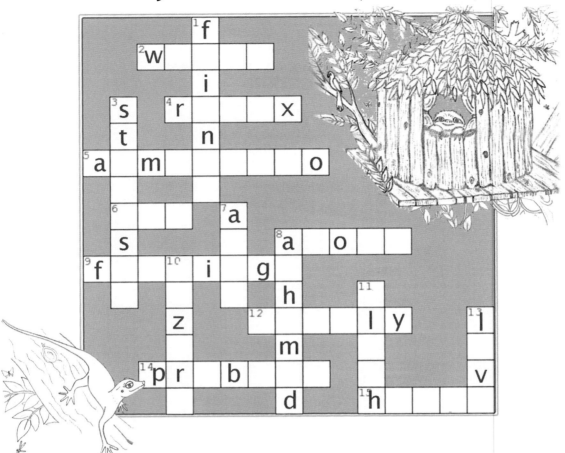

Clues Across

2: Be anxious (5)
4: De-stress, chill out (5)
5: Anna is one of these (9)
5: The name of the sloth (3)
8: All by yourself (5)
9: Emotions, sensations (8)
12 : The people you live with
14 : Difficulty, something to solve
15 : Glad, joyful (5)

Clues Down

1: People you like to spend time with (7)
3: Anxious, worried (8)
7: The name of the armadillo (4)
8: Sorry, embarrassed (7)
10: Livy is one of these (6)
11: Sam is one of these (5)
13 : the name of the lizard (4)

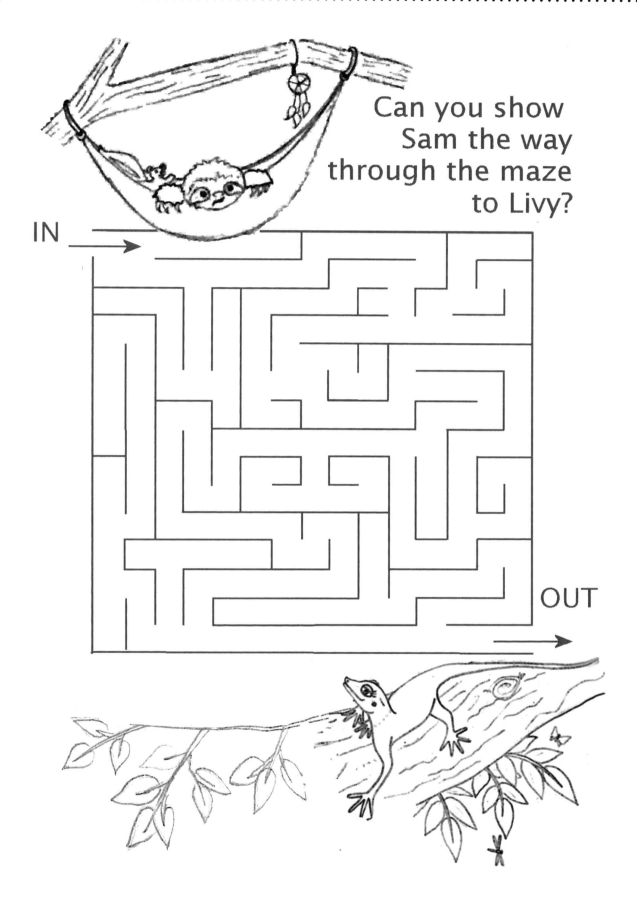

Can you show
Sam the way
through the maze
to Livy?

IN

OUT

Sam's Word Search
Can you find all the words?

```
Z S T R E S S E D N X R K I K
A N I L D W S S L D F G D A B
N U J V T S K P H P H V M R P
N O R Y D G L F R N S Y O A T
A L N B P N O O D K L R Q V J
D L H W V I B V I I P R L Y R
Y I Z B N L B A M W O O S R D
V D U V E E M A M F A W E Z S
I A H M V E F Y C S X L V G F
L M S A M F H E H P A L N S N
F R E J P T D A F X E K C U X
F A G O O P M X L D R A Z I L
O T F L U E Y B S P N D S W B
K A S S D N E I R F K C H O G
T L M C P L E H T U I D D W C
```

SAM	LIZARD	FAMILY
SLOTH	STRESSED	RELAX
ANNA	HAPPY	WORRY
ARMADILLO	FEELINGS	ASHAMED
LIVY	FRIENDS	PROBLEM
	HELP	

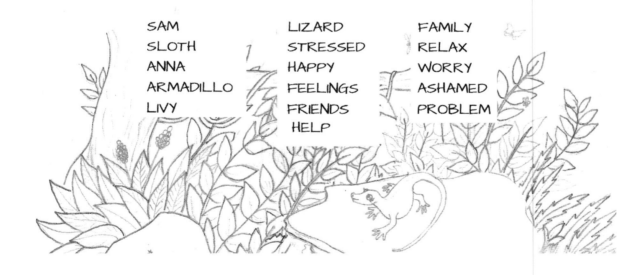

There are ten differences between these two pictures.
Can you find them all?

ANSWER: D   A   B   C   **D**   E

Sam wants to climb back up to
the sloths' tree top home.
Which vine should Sam use?
A, B, C, D or E?

Sammy Sloth's Crossword - ANSWERS

The crossword grid contains the following answers:

2 Across: worry
4 Across: relax
5 Across: armadillo
6 Across: sam
8 Across: alone
9 Across: feelings
12 Across: family
14 Across: problem
15 Across: happy

1 Down: friends
3 Down: stressed
7 Down: anna
8 Down: ashamed
10 Down: lizard
11 Down: sloth
13 Down: livy

Clues Across

2: Be anxious (5)
4: De-stress, chill out (5)
5: Anna is one of these (9)
5: The name of the sloth (3)
8: All by yourself (5)
9: Emotions, sensations (8)
12 : The people you live with
14 : Difficulty, something to solve
15 : Glad, joyful (5)

Clues Down

1: People you like to spend time with (7)
3: Anxious, worried (8)
7: The name of the armadillo (4)
8: Sorry, embarrassed (7)
10: Livy is one of these (6)
11: Sam is one of these (5)
13 : the name of the lizard (4)

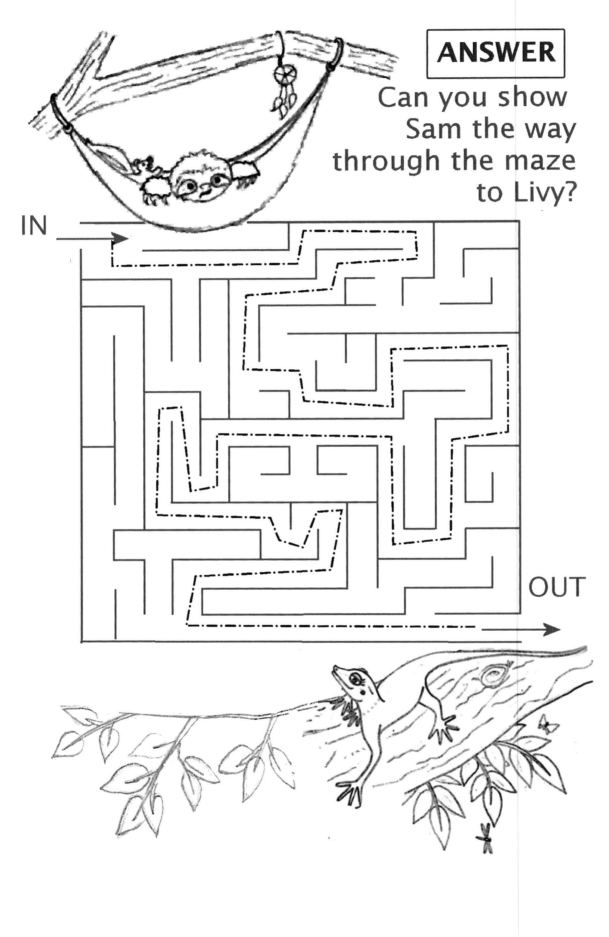

ANSWER

Can you show Sam the way through the maze to Livy?

IN

OUT

Sam's Word Search
ANSWERS

```
Z S T R E S S E D N X R K I   K
A N I L D W S S L D F G D A   B
N U J V T S K P H P H V M R   P
N O R Y D G L F R N S Y O A   T
A L N B P N O O D K L R Q V   J
D L H W V I B V I I P R L Y   R
Y I Z B N L B A M W O O S R   D
V D U V E E M A M F A W E Z   S
I A H M V E F Y C S X L V G   F
L M S A M F H E H P A L N S   N
F R E J P T D A F X E K C U   X
F A G O O P M X L D R A Z I   L
O T F L U E Y B S P N D S W   B
K A S S D N E I R F K C H O   G
T L M C P L E H T U I D D W   C
```

SAM	LIZARD	FAMILY
SLOTH	STRESSED	RELAX
ANNA	HAPPY	WORRY
ARMADILLO	FEELINGS	ASHAMED
LIVY	FRIENDS	PROBLEM
	HELP	

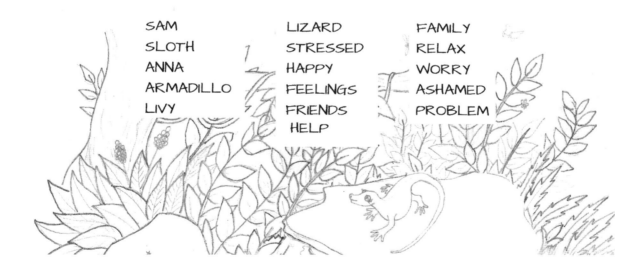

There are ten differences between these two pictures.
ANSWERS

Chapter 14

Sammy Sloth's Board Game

NOTES AND ADVICE WHEN PLAYING THE BOARD GAME

The questions are designed to vary in terms of difficulty to allow some children answer some questions unaided. This can be useful not only in consolidating the story but maintaining or improving confidence.

More complicated questions are included which may be answered by older or more able children and they may do so unaided but others may require discussion and support from supportive adults. It may be that discussing and talking through the question is enough to generate a sufficient answer or it might be that the child will have to refer back to the book to find the answer. Either method is acceptable as the goal is to acquire a better understanding of the narrative and underlying themes of the book. It is hoped that by truly understanding: the story, its characters, their behaviour, and how that impacts on them and others, they will be able to apply and relate the thoughts, feelings and emotions of the characters and their situations to their own lives and struggles. Reading a book about others experiencing similar difficulties not only normalises their thoughts feelings and actions but opens a dialogue around these issues and helps them to formulate plans and to think of ways to cope and seek support in their own life.

Please copy the questions below onto the game cards overleaf, the game cards should then be split 50/50 across the two shaded/coloured boxes on the game board. These form the basis of the game and all players should start on Sammy Sloth. A colour version of this game is available online as an eResource.

QUESTIONS FOR SAMMY SLOTH'S BOARD GAME

Where does Sammy live? (move 2 places)

Why is Sammy is worried? (move 3 spaces)

How do we know Sammy is worried? (move 3 places)

What does Sammy feel like he has in his pants? (move 1 space)

Who is Sammy is comforted by? (move 3 spaces)

Why is Sammy is embarrassed? (move 3 spaces)

How did Livy helped? (move 3 spaces)

How did Livy know Sammy needed help? (move 2 spaces)

Was Anna kind? (move 2 spaces)

Do you think Anna made Sammy feel better? If not why? (move 3 spaces)

Do you think Anna understood how Sammy felt? (move 3 spaces)

What did Anna advise Sammy to do? (move 2 spaces)

Was Anna's advice helpful? (move 3 spaces)

What does Livy suggest to help Sammy? (move 3 spaces)

Was Livy's advice helpful? (move 3 spaces)

Do you think Sammy felt better at the end? (move 3 spaces)

What type of creature is Anna (move 1 space)

What type of creature is Sammy? (move one space)

What type of creature is Livy? (move one space)

What did Sammy think he was sitting on? (move 2 spaces)

Find three words or phrases that tell us that Sammy is worried (move 3 spaces)

How do you think Sammy felt at the end of the story?

Do you think Livy is kind? How do you know this? (move 3 spaces)

What did Sammy feel in his tummy? (move 2 spaces)

Sammy did something to make his feet hurt, what did he do? (move 2 spaces)

What rushed around Sammy's head? (move 1 space)

What are sloths usually like? (move 3 spaces)

Was Sammy different to how sloths usually are? (move 3 spaces)

Did something in particular happen to make Sammy worried? (move 3 spaces)

Anna told Sammy he has no need to worry as he had lots of good things in his life, what were those things? (move 3 spaces)

What did Livy tell Sammy about worrying, is he the only person in the world who worries? (move 3 spaces)

What helps to ease worries? (move 3 spaces)

Is it ok and normal to worry? (move 3 spaces)

Will worrying feeling last forever? (move 2 spaces)

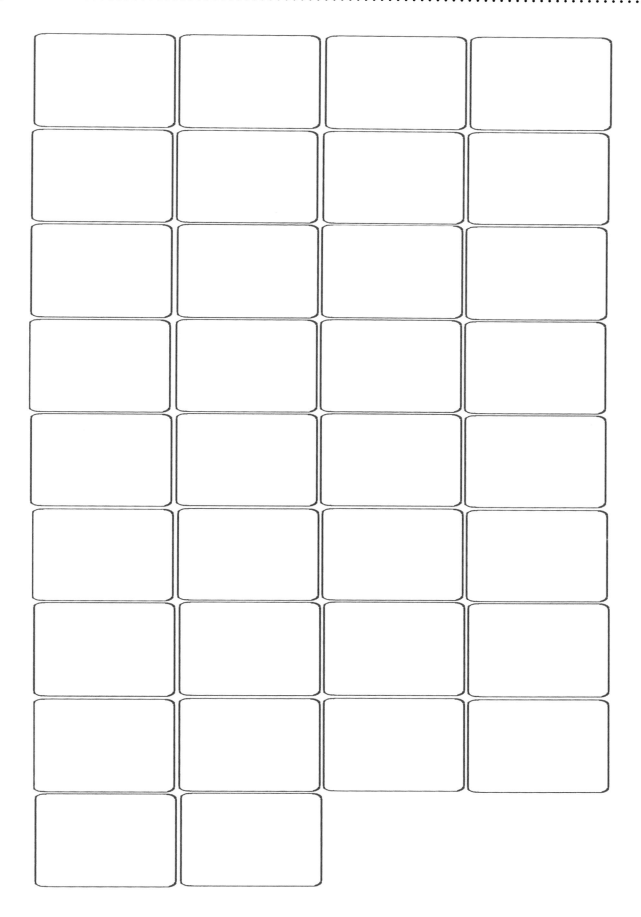

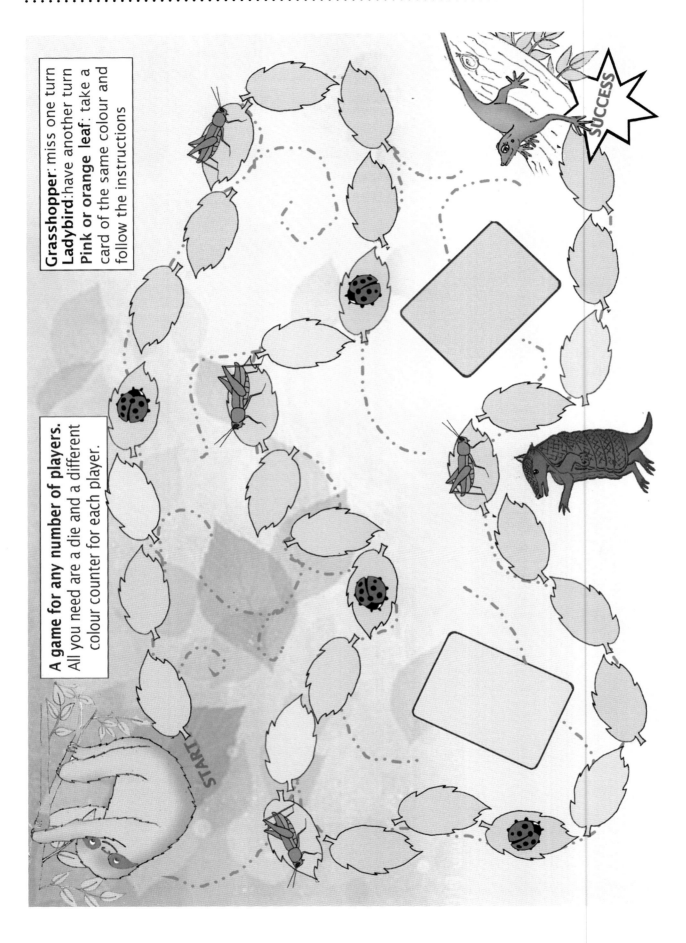

Grasshopper: miss one turn
Ladybird: have another turn
Pink or orange leaf: take a card of the same colour and follow the instructions

A game for any number of players.
All you need are a die and a different colour counter for each player.

START

SUCCESS

Chapter 15

What happens next?

◆   Draw, use crafts or continue to write the story.

◆   Do things turn out well for the characters?

◆   How has what has happened affected them?

◆   Draw, use crafts or continue to write the story.

Chapter 16

Alternate ending?

◆ Draw, use crafts or re-write the ending of Sammy's story.

◆ Do things still turn out well for the characters?

◆ What happens instead?

◆